Qi Gong

stand

exercises

including the 5
animal positions

Hartmut von Czapski

Photos Ellen and Hartmut von Czapski

Hartmut von Czapski

Qi Gong
stand
exercises

including the 5
animal positions

Imprint

Bibliographic information from the German National Library:
The German National Library lists this publication in the German
National Bibliography; detailed bibliographical data can be found on
the Internet at http://dnb.dnb.de.
© 2019 Hartmut von Czapski
Production and publishing: BoD - Books on Demand, Norderstedt
ISBN: 9783751907323

Qi Gong stand exercises

Content :

About the author

Hartmut von Czapski

Non-medical practitioner since 1984. Since 1987 exercise of acupuncture (Teacher Fr.Dr. Li Te, Chief Physician Nankei Clinic). Several stays in China with professional trainings.
1987 Scientific training of Uni.Tübingen passed: "Ecology and its biological basis".
Since1990 seminars, yoga and Qi Gong courses at various institutes.
Since 1990 more than 1000 Qi Gong classes have been held.
Qi Gong Teacher 49009 des Mi Gong Rulai Buddhist Center for Qi Gong, Shanghai.
Training to Qi Gong Therapeut by Prof. Wu, Shanghai. Lectures at the Medica in Dusseldorf on the treatment of incontinence with T.C.M .
1999 acupuncture specialist training for dentists; Teacher activity on various therapies.

Teaching Qi Gong Forms:

Medical Qi Gong according to Prof.Wu.

Taiji Qigong after Li Ding.

Ten meditations on the mountain Wudang.

The Eighteenfold Method of Exercise.

The "Movements of the 5 Animals".

Qi Gong after Guo Lin for immune boosting.

The "Eight elegant exercises. "

"Wai dan gung"

"Tai Hu Lake Qi Gong"

Tai Chi for beginners by Dr. med. Jiang Hao-quan.

And much more.

Qi Gong

Qi Gong

The term "Qi Gong" includes various types of exercises to absorb the "Qi", the life energy, and let it flow in the energy channels, the so-called "meridians". It is a substance that you normally do not see and grope, but can feel. The ancient Chinese philosophers thought that Qi is a source substance that originated in the Big Bang.

According to the Chinese view, Qi is a continuously moving and active substance, the basic substance from which the body originates. Qi receives the human life functions. By definition Qi in Qi Gong is an "essence" substance in the body with a certain energy. Qi can be formed, developed, transformed and moved in the body. Breathing moves the energy in the meridians. But even after a long practice of Qi Gong, one can move and absorb qi with the mind in the body.

These body and breathing exercises have at least a 4000-year-old tradition in China, as can be seen in descriptions of funerary offerings. There are many different types of exercises. On the one hand the soft Qi Gong, which contains many meditative elements based on the imagination and is often performed while sitting or lying down. On the other hand, we know the hard Qi Gong, which also strengthens the muscles and tendons and massages the internal organs. Think e.g. to the achievements of the Shaolin monks in Kung Fu or to the acrobatic skills of the actors of Peking Opera. But Qigong exercises not only strengthen the body, but also calm the mind and regulate the autonomic nervous system.

A special form is the therapeutic qigong, which prescribes certain exercises for certain illnesses. Like any empirical science, qigong is always being developed. For example, in recent decades, e.g. certain new exercises against cancer are famous for their good results (Qi Gong after Guo Lin for improving the immune system). The high blood pressure research institute Shanghai has already published in 1978 works with reports on changes that causes Qigong on the ECG and EEG. Work has also been published that our sympathetic nervous system, which is active through prolonged stress, achieves relaxation through Qi Gong by predominance of the parasympathetic nervous system.

In China, in many hospitals, in addition to the Department of Medicine, there is a Department of Traditional Chinese Medicine. This includes the treatment room for the Qi Gong therapist. Here the patient is not only taught exercises that he should practice regularly at home, the therapist also supplies the patient with energy that he himself has absorbed. Training to become a Qi Gong therapist is usually tedious. After 5 years of practice, you can teach Qi Gong exercises and also treat after 10 years. Mr. von Czapski has been trained by Prof.Wu as a Qi Gong therapist

Important energy centers

"Real" Dantian. It lies between the navel and the spine.

Lower Dantian, about 2 fingers wide under the navel. Approx. at the acupuncture point "Qi Hai", sea of energy.

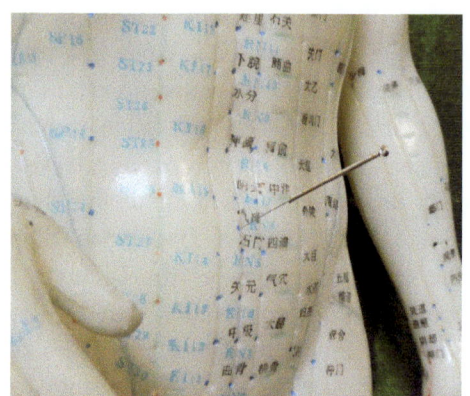

Middle Dantian, heart center. At the level of a hollow on the sternum, between the nipples. Tan Zhong (KG17) ..

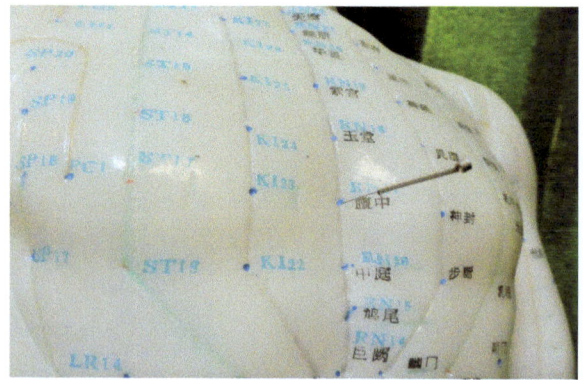

Upper Dantian, Yintang. Between the eyebrows, just above the Nasal root.

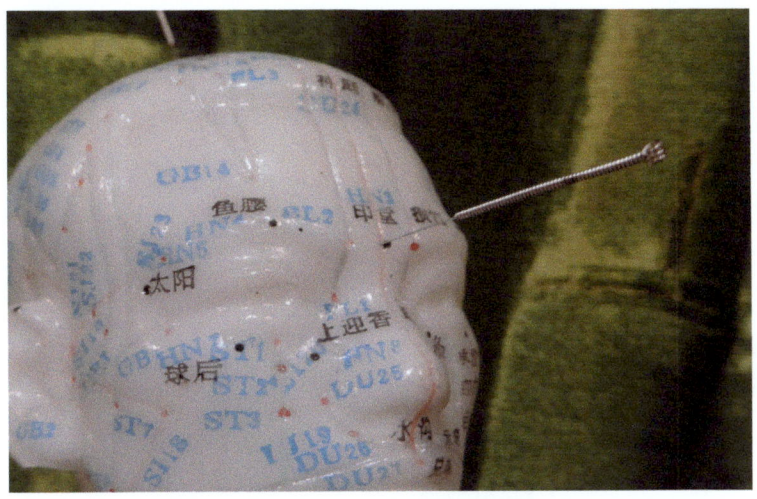

Hui Yen, KG1. In the middle of the perineum, between the anus and Genital organs

Energy intake and delivery points

<u>Yongchuan.</u> When we "claw the toes" a hollow is created below the base toe joints. Point kidney 1.

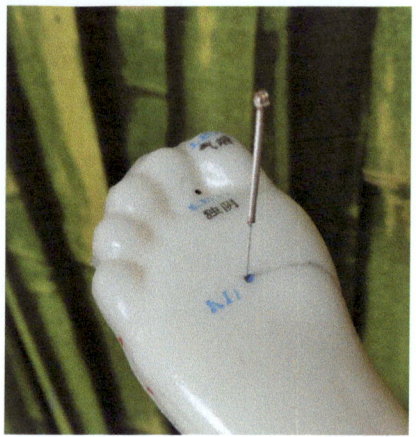

<u>Laogong.</u> If we tip the tip of the ring finger into the palm of our hand, we come to this point.

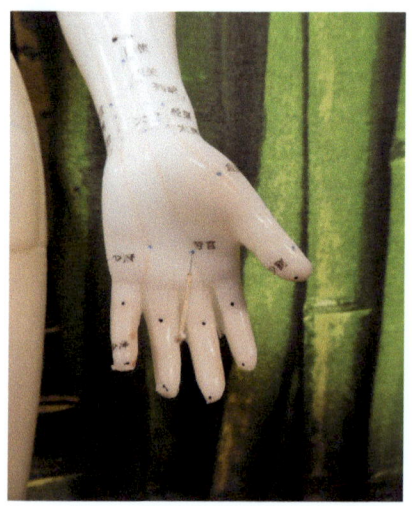

Bai Hui. Located in the middle of an imaginary line between the tips of the ears in a small hollow.

Mingmen. If you put the top of your index finger under the back of your costal arch and stretch your thumb towards your spine, you can use your thumb tips to reach the Mingmen point on the spine.

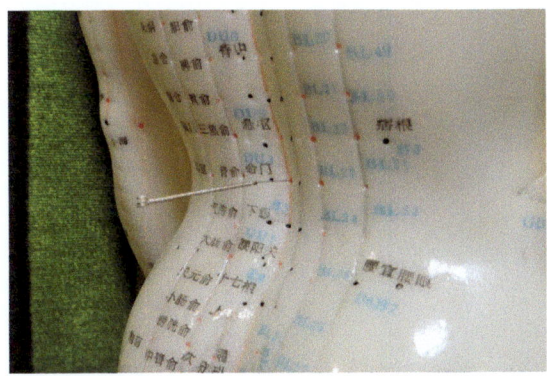

The breathing

Breathing should flow calmly and regularly, deep but relaxed and harmonious. Anyone who has practiced abdominal breathing several times can also do this during the standing exercises. It should flow so naturally that you no longer have to pay attention to it. The focus should not be on breathing but on the energy centers and points.

With abdominal breathing, you stretch your stomach slightly forward when inhaling and pull it in slightly when exhaling. You only breathe with your stomach, not with your chest. Has a relaxing effect and strengthens the Qi in the Dantian. Beginners should practice sitting or lying down. It is helpful to put one hand on your stomach and the other on your chest the first time.

Basic position

Stand feet shoulder-width apart and parallel.

Bend your knees slightly, but not beyond the tips of your feet.

Tilt the pelvis forward and down so that the lumbar spine straightens. For people with a hollow back, this is often difficult at the beginning, the upper body leans back. This should be straightened out.

The spine should be as straight as possible.

The chin is lowered slightly, the cervical spine is stretched.

All nerve impulses can flow more freely.

Take your shoulders back, then let your arms hang loosely. Relax your shoulders. Move your elbows slightly to the side. This creates some space in the armpits.
The hands are not stretched, loose, but slightly stretched in the palms to absorb energy. Light, involuntary Finger movements are a good sign when it comes to energy consumption.
We can imagine that the feet, like the roots of a tree, reach deep. The upper body is movable like the branches of a tree without giving up the basic position described above.

19

Try to calm down, to absorb nature and the life energy in it. In addition, the inner mindset should be like an empty white room.

Always check your position; Tilt your pelvis, loosen your knees, etc.

You should try to stay in this position for 5 minutes at the beginning. To do this, we can look into nature and possibly hear a calm piece of music that lasts 5 minutes. After a few days you can increase the duration of the exercise. The duration is unlimited.

Bending your arms or legs causes a slight build-up of energy. Imagine a large water pipe that opens into a smaller one, the flow rate is increased. The meridians are flushed out, so to speak.

You may feel a tremor in your muscles. It is perfectly normal. Blood and qi want to make their way. It is a good sign. If it gets too strong, stop the exercise and walk around loosening your arms and legs.
This exercise improves health, calms the mind, the life energy flows more freely and is strengthened. Even if you only practice this basic level every day, this has a positive effect on your physical and mental health.
In the classic of the yellow emperor "Nei Jing" from the time of the fighting empires, it is written: "Serene and wishless (be), real energy in the flow, keeping the mind inside, then no illness comes. With breathing qi (absorb), concentrate on yourself , keep the mind; relax all muscles.

A peculiarity of Qi Gong as a practice method is that you have to enter an inner state of exercise. Posture and movements and breathing work together, mind and body are relaxed or tense, the thoughts are concentrated and used. All this intensifies and regulates every organ function and stimulates the body's energy potential. The effect is keeping the body healthy, preventing illness and a long life.

In many exercise series, it is advisable to hold the basic stand, or one of the other stand positions, between the individual exercise parts for 1-2 minutes. You can feel the effect of the previous exercise or redistribute the energy that was created.

All of the following exercises are based on the basic position.

<u>Earth position.</u> Extend your hands diagonally forward. At the level of the lower Dantian.

Absorb earth energy with the Laogong points, through which arms and body lead. Possibly, associated with inhalation. Derive energy used in the ground via the Yongchuan points. Possibly, associated with an exhalation.

Cleaning and energy consumption.

Lower tree position

Hold your arms in a circle in front of your lower abdomen, as if you were hugging a tree. The fingertips are directed towards each other and about 3 transverse fingers apart. The palms of your hands are directed towards the lower Dantian.

We find our way back to our center. Calm strength. Against high blood pressure with regular exercise.

Upper tree position.

Hold your arms forward, the palms of your hands pointing towards the heart center, as if you were hugging a tree. The fingertips are directed towards each other and about 3 transverse fingers apart. Let the elbows hang down so far that the shoulders relax.

The heart center is stimulated. For low blood pressure and fatigue. For high blood pressure and heart disease, do not use for more than 1-2 minutes.

Kuanyin position.

Hold your right hand in front of your right shoulder, your elbow close to your body. The fingertips of the thumb and index finger touch each other. The inside of the hand is facing forward.

The left hand is in front of the lower Dantian. The palm of the bowl is facing upwards. The fingertips of the thumb and middle finger touch each other.

Creates more inner harmony and is health-promoting.

Stick-hold position.

Hold your right hand in front of the solar plexus as if you were holding a stick vertically. The left hand is held in a bowl shape in front of the lower Dantian.

When we look through the upper hand, we look exactly in the middle of the palm of the lower hand.

Concentration on the palms.

Has a stabilizing effect. Energy in the lower Dantian is increased.

River position.

Imagine yourself standing in a stream. Large gymnastic balls are to your right and left. Extend your hands sideways down to the level of the lower Dantian, as if you were holding these balls in the stream. Focus on the Laogong points. Strong energy absorption over the Laogong points.

Heart position.

The hands are folded in such a way that the thumbs lie against each other between the index fingers. The little fingers are tightly closed. A hollow forms between the hands.

The hands are held in front of the heart center. Concentration on the palms and the area of the heart. 1-2 minutes. Acts on heart and cordiality.

Crane position.

Place your knees side by side. Put one foot forward and extend your knee. The back knee is bent. The main weight is on the back leg. It is important that both knees are level and next to each other. You can also change your leg after a few minutes. Hold your arms in a ring in front of your torso. As if you were holding a large ball. The palms of your hands point in the direction Tanzhong (heart center). The fingertips point towards each other and are about 3 transverse finger widths apart.
Look ahead. Shoulders loose, hands loose, elbows slightly lowered. A position that requires some practice. However, a strong energy intake is the reward. Pressure equalization between the top and the bottom. Recommended for Qi Gong teachers or therapists.

Energy intake from nature

Feet shoulder width, parallel. Put your left foot forward, knees straight.

The right leg is the supporting leg, knees bent.

Hold your left hand next to your left thigh, palm facing forward.

Hold your right hand next to your right shoulder, palm facing forward.

Imagine that with the right hand (Laogong) one absorbs energy from the moon, sun or a tree and releases it with the lower hand.

Energy spiral

Basic position

Imagine that you inhale good energy via Bai Hui and spiral down, clockwise, down to the navel height (Mingmen height).

Guide the energy used during exhalation spirally, clockwise over the soles of the feet (Yongchuan) into the ground.

The body may vibrate slightly.

Luohan exercise.

1) Basic position.

Place one hand, palm straight up, on Dantian.

Place one hand upright, palm to the side, with your thumb on the heart center (Tanzhong).

Keep your eyes on the upper middle finger.

The energy rises. Not suitable for hypertensives (RR over 160).

Luohan exercise 2

Exercise 1, then point your upper hand down. Thumb remains on Thanzhong.

Hold the lower hand in a bowl shape in front of the Dantian.

Hold an imaginary energy ball.

Improves the quality of Qi, strengthens the heart and lungs.

For advanced users: Wide, lower position. Keep your back straight. Luohan position 1: Hold lower hand in front of the gender. Shell-shaped upwards. Hold your upper hand in front of your face. Palm to the side.

For Luohan position 2: Hold the lower hand in front of the sex, the upper hand in front of the neck. Hold a large imaginary ball.

Energy ball

Basic position
Hold your hands loosely under the Dantian. The tips of the thumb touch.
Imagine a glowing rotating ball. Enhances the energy absorption in the Laogong points and storage in the Dantian.

<u>Yin and Yang exercise.</u>

Basic status

At the level of the Dantian, place your hands straight and parallel above each other. But they don't touch. Only the tips of the thumb touch.

Balancing yin and yang, right and left. Focus on the space between your fingers.

Eagle exercise

Turn your feet outwards. The tips of the toes point outwards. The inside of the feet stand forward in an imaginary line. The knees bent. Form two strongly bent eagle beaks with your fingers. All fingertips together. Hold your hands on your right and left, diagonally outwards, in front of your shoulders.

The qi gathers in the hands. The qi flow is improved, the meridians connect. Running can improve, the yin meridians of the legs are strengthened. But yin and yang are balanced.

The 5 animals stand positions Wu Xing Gong

These exercises are based on the Wu Xin Xi movement system
(Art of 5 animals) to Hua Tuo. He was a famous doctor of the
Eastern Han Dynasty (until about 220 AD). The 5 imitated animals
are:

Tiger, deer, bear, monkey and crane.

The tiger is the king of the forest, powerful and strong.

The deer is smart, runs quickly and easily.

The bear is powerful and calm.

The monkey is smart and lovable.

The crane is calm and relaxed.

These exercises are also good for children between 5 and 15 years
old.

They promote intelligence, the immune system, the functions of
the internal organs and strengthen the muscles and tendons. The
flow of qi and blood is promoted. Yin and yang harmonized. The
self-healing powers are stimulated.

Monkey position.

Place your left foot on the ball of your toes. The right foot lies completely.

Bend your knees. Shift the weight to the right leg.

Bend your fingers and hold them together. The left hand next to the head.

The right hand points with the palm and fingers to point Liver 13 on the lower costal arch.

Straighten your head and pull your neck back.

The eyes look up and down and to the right and left.

For 3-5 minutes

Promotes the Qi and blood flow of the whole digestive system and the eye muscles.

Deer position.

Put your left foot forward, put your right foot back. Bend your knees.
Claw your toes in the ground. Shift the weight to the center.
Bend the middle index and ring fingers. Put your thumbs over your ears to your head. Stretch your head, take your chin back.
3-5 min.
Acts on the digestion, the lungs, the yin and yang balance. Boosts brain energy.

Bear position.

Slight tackle, knees slightly bent. The toes claw into the ground.
Bear claws form, fingers together. Bend your arms in your elbows
and hold the claws of your bear next to your shoulders.
Take back chin.
Good for the cervical spine and brain energy.

Tiger position.

Put your left foot far forward so that your thigh is horizontal. Claw your toes in the ground. Shift the weight slightly forward. Form Tiger Claws. Hold the left claw in front of your face, palm facing forward. Place the right one with your thumb on the right belt line, palm facing down. Yin energy is collected, Qi flows into the belt meridian (Daimai).

Open your eyes wide. Look through the tiger claw.

Strengthens the body, the Qi intake, the internal organs and the Qi flow in the 12 meridians.

Crane position.

Only put your left foot on your toes. Shift your weight slightly to the right, but also to the front of your toes, bend your knees. The Qi flow of the legs is strengthened.
Bend your upper body slightly forward. Hands and arms loosely forward in a circle. Like two wings that the crane holds forward. Fingertips facing each other and down. Qi is collected in the hands and continues to flow into the chest
Extend your head and chin up.
3-5 min.

More books from the author

Taiji Qi Gong ISBN:9783752820072
In this book there are 22 Taiji Qi Gong exercises described. These exercises improve energy intake, strengthen the self-healing powers and bring about a balance of the vegetative nervous system. They promote concentration and inner peace. They have a positive effect on the digestive organs, the muscles, the tendons, joints and the spine. The increased oxygen intake strengthens the heart and lungs.

Qi Gong sitting ISBN: 9783750431409
This book describes 34 Qi Gong exercises performed while sitting. From simple movement exercises to Tuina massage exercises, breathing exercises and concentration exercises. These exercises improve the energy intake, strengthen the self-healing powers and balance the autonomic nervous system. They promote the ability to concentrate and inner peace. They have a positive effect on the digestive system, the muscles, the tendons, joints and the spine. The increased oxygen intake strengthens the heart and lungs.

It is very well suited as a exercise book for occupational medicine, for old people's home, as a com pletion for any Qi Gong course or just for in between for all office or computer workers. The many photos and the clear description make it easy to understand the exercises.

Medical Qi Gong according to Prof. Wu ISBN 9783751904575
This book shows exercises that include have an excellent effect on the following symptoms: high and low blood pressure, stomach and intestinal complaints, lung problems, insomnia, nervousness, lack of concentration, lack of energy, back pain and excessive stress.

With regular and persistent practice of Qi Gong, practitioners can improve their health and find inner peace and relaxation. Since the exercises can be carried out with different levels of effort, they are also suitable for older, weakened people.